Ants

Edited by Heather C. Hudak

Published by Weigl Publishers Inc.
350 5th Avenue, Suite 3304, PMB 6G
New York, NY 10118-0069
Website: www.weigl.com

Library of Congress Cataloging-in-Publication Data available upon request.
Fax 1-866-44-WEIGL for the attention of the Publishing Records department.

ISBN 978-1-59036-862-6 (hard cover)
ISBN 978-1-59036-863-3 (soft cover)

Printed in the United States of America
1 2 3 4 5 6 7 8 9 0 12 11 10 09 08

Editor: Heather C. Hudak
Design: Terry Paulhus

Weigl acknowledges Getty Images as its image supplier for this title.

All of the Internet URLs given in the book were valid at the time of publication. However, due to the dynamic nature of the Internet, some addresses may have changed, or sites may have ceased to exist since publication. While the author and publisher regret any inconvenience this may cause readers, no responsibility for any such changes can be accepted by either the author or the publisher.

Every reasonable effort has been made to trace ownership and to obtain permission to reprint copyright material. The publishers would be pleased to have any errors or omissions brought to their attention so that they may be corrected in subsequent printings.

CONTENTS

What is an Ant?

Have you ever seen a group of small creatures working together? These may be ants. Ants are a type of insect. There are at least 20,000 types of ant in the world.

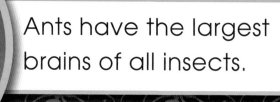

Ants have the largest brains of all insects.

5

6

Back in Time

Did you know that ants have been living on Earth for more than 100 million years? They can be found almost everywhere on the planet.

Ants today look much like ants that lived millions of years ago.

Ant Life Cycle

Ants begin life inside small, oval eggs. Wormlike **larvae** hatch from the eggs. The larvae have no eyes or legs. They shed their skin many times as they grow.

Larvae become **pupae**. They spin a silklike **cocoon** around their body. Inside the cocoon, the pupae change into ants.

Ants can live for many years, or they can have a short life. Some ants live for less than one year, and other types can live for more than 10 years.

Eggs

Feeding larvae

Pupae

Adult

9

What Does an Ant Look Like?

What does your body look like? It is quite different from an ant's body. Like all insects, ants have a head, **thorax**, and **abdomen**. They have six legs attached to their thorax.

The head consists of the jaws, eyes, and **antennae**. An ant's eyes are made up of many lenses. These help the ants see movement very well. The antennae allow the ants to smell, touch, taste, and hear.

Adult ants are between 0.07 and 1 inch (2 and 25 millimeters) long.

head

thorax

abdomen

To Serve and Protect

Ants have poison sacks or stingers at the end of their abdomen. They use these to protect themselves against **predators**.

Army ants bite and sting any creatures that come nearby. They will even bite a huge snake!

Ants can carry up to 20 times their own weight.

Above and Beyond

Have you ever seen a flying ant? These ants have two pairs of wings. The front wings of a flying ant are much larger than the back wings. Ants use their wings to fly short distances.

Flying ants only fly during the summer months. This is when the ants mate.

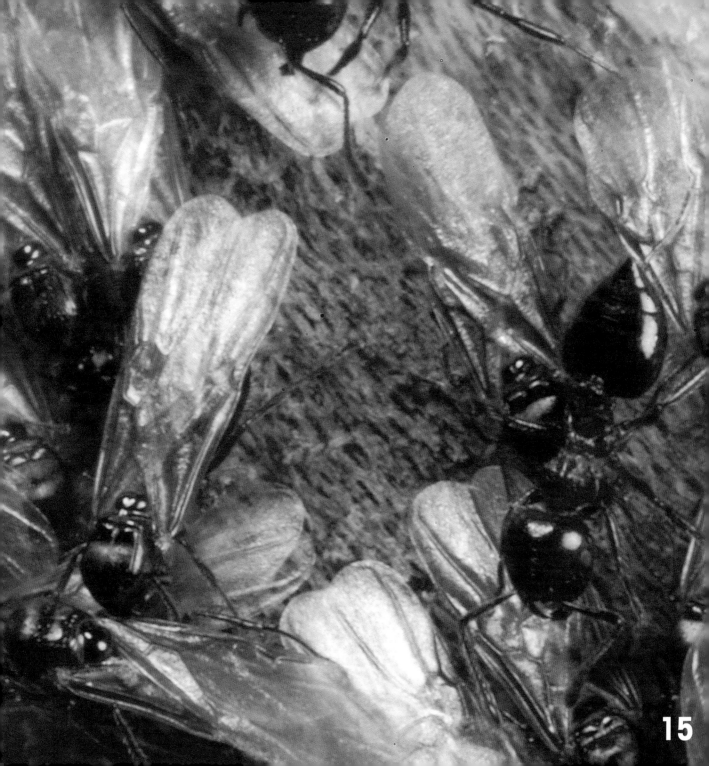

15

What's for Dinner?

What if you had two stomachs? Ants have one stomach to hold food for themselves, and one that holds food for their family. An ant stores food in its stomach until it reaches its family. Then, the ant spits out the food for the other ants to eat. Many ants eat small insects, as well as fruits and vegetables.

Some ants keep herds of aphids. Aphids are tiny insects that feed on the sap of plants. A hungry ant will rub the back of an aphid with its antennae. This will make a drop of honeydew for the ant to eat. In return, ants protect aphids from predators.

17

Home Sweet Home

Imagine if you lived in a house with thousands of other people. Ants live in **colonies** with thousands of other ants.

Colonies are made up of many rooms and tunnels under the ground. Most ants live in the soil. Some live in wood. Others live in holes made inside plants, such as acorns and twigs.

Anthills form when ants are digging out the colony. The hills are made up of dirt, sand, clay, and dead leaves left near the entrance to the colony.

19

Insect Lore

People around the world have legends and myths about ants. In some places, people believe that ants are **messengers**.

When ants move their eggs and climb to higher ground, some people believe this means there will be rain very soon.

Ants may make their colony inside the door of a house. Some people think this means that the home owner will be blessed with good luck.

Draw an Ant

Supplies:
cardboard egg carton, paint, four long pipe cleaners, markers, scissors

1. Use three cups from a cardboard egg carton to form the body of an ant.

2. Paint the cups.

3. Next, poke a hole on both sides of the first cup. Thread the pipe cleaner through the holes so that the ends stick out at the top. These are the ant's antennae.

4. Then, poke three more holes on each side of the second cup. Thread a pipe cleaner through each hole to make the ant's legs.

5. Draw eyes on the front cup.

6. Now you have a colorful egg-carton ant!

Find Out More

To find out more about ants, visit these sites.

AntWeb
www.antweb.org

The Ants
www.earthlife.net/insects/
ants.html

Ants
www.zoomschool.com/
subjects/insects/ant

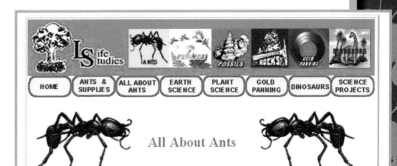

All About Ants

Ants have been living on the Earth for more than 100 million years and can be found almost anywhere on the planet. It is estimated that there are about 20,000 different species of ants. For this reason ants have been called Earth's most successful species.

Ants build many different types of homes. Many ants build simple little mounds out of dirt or sand. Other ants use small sticks mixed with dirt and sand to make a stronger mound that offers protection from rain. Western Harvester ants make a small mound on top, but then tunnel up to **15 feet** straight down to hibernate during winter. Ant mounds consist of many chambers connected by tunnels. Different chambers are used for nurseries, food storage, and resting places for the worker ants. Some ants live in wood like termites. Army ants don't make a home at all but travel in large groups searching for food.

Sociology: Ants are social insects, which means they live in large colonies or groups. Some colonies consist of millions of ants. There are three types of ants in each species, the queen, the sterile female workers, and males. The male ants only serve one purpose, to mate with future queen ants and do not live very long. The queen grows to adulthood, mates, and then spends the rest of her life laying eggs. A colony may have only one queen, or there may be many queens depending on the species. Ants go through four stages of development: egg, larva, pupa, and adult.

Anatomy: Ants have three main parts. The head, the trunk(middle section), and the rear or metasoma. All six legs are attached to the trunk. The head consists of the jaws, eyes, and antennae. The eyes of ants are made up of many lenses enabling them to see movement very well. The antennae are special organs of smell, touch, taste, and hearing. The metasoma contains the stomach and rectum. Many species of ants have poison sacks and/or stingers in the end of the metasoma for defense against their many predators. To see a diagram and learn more about ant anatomy visit our Ant Anatomy page.

Organs: Ants do not have lungs. Oxygen enters through tiny holes all over the body and Carbon Dioxide leaves through the same holes. There are no blood vessels. The heart is a long tube that pumps colorless blood from the head back to the rear and then back up to the head again. The blood kind of coats the insides of the ants and is then sucked into the tube and pumped up to the head again. The nervous system of ants consists of a long nerve cord that also runs from head to rear with branches leading to the parts of the body, kind of like a human spinal cord.

FEATURE SITE:
www.infowest.com/
life/aants.htm

Glossary

abdomen: part of body which has digestive and reproductive organs

antennae: long, thin body parts that extend from an insect's head

cocoon: a silky case spun by young insects for protection

colonies: groups that live together

larvae: young insects

messengers: ants who carry messages to others

predators: animals that hunt other animals for food

pupae: a young insect before it becomes an adult

thorax: part of body between neck and abdomen

Index